Contents

The author, left, sets up camp in a remote meadow in Tasmania.
Fullerton Images

BACKPACKER®

The 10 Essentials of Outdoor Gear
WHAT YOU NEED TO STAY ALIVE

Kristin Hostetter

FALCONGUIDES

GUILFORD, CONNECTICUT
HELENA, MONTANA

AN IMPRINT OF GLOBE PEQUOT PRESS

To buy books in quantity for corporate use
or incentives, call **(800) 962–0973**
or e-mail **premiums@GlobePequot.com**.

FALCONGUIDES®

Backpacker is a registered trademark of Cruz Bay Publishing, Inc.
FalconGuides is an imprint of Globe Pequot Press.
Falcon, FalconGuides, and Outfit Your Mind are registered trademarks of Morris
Book Publishing, LLC.

Text design: Sheryl P. Kober
Layout: Sue Murray
Project editor: Julie Marsh

Library of Congress Cataloging-in-Publication Data is available.
ISBN 978-0-7627-8266-6

Printed in the United States of America
10 9 8 7 6 5 4 3 2 1

PREFACE

With all due respect to the celebrated "official" list of 10 Essentials that the Mountaineers (a Seattle-based outing club) first published in 1930s, surviving in the outdoors in dire emergencies has little to do with packing a handy kit of gadgets. Sure, having the right tools for any job makes things a lot easier and amps up your chances for success. And that's what this book is all about. But surviving in the outdoors is really about staying calm, controlling your emotions, using ingenuity, and being creative with the tools you have at hand to keep you alive until you either rescue yourself or someone else does.

I've talked to so many survival experts over the course of my almost twenty years working at *Backpacker* magazine, and I have a guilty fascination with any and every survival show I can find on cable TV. I've spent a whole lot of time in the wilderness, but I've never been in severely dire straits. Maybe that's because I'm lucky. But maybe it's because I've learned how to pack properly, so I'm ready for any situation.

This book's goal is to help you be more prepared. Whether you get lost and stuck out there an extra day or two, get slammed by a freak snowstorm in July, slip on a mossy log and tweak your ankle, or take an unexpected swim during an icy river crossing, having the right stuff—and the smarts to know how to use it—will help you get out of any bind. I've identified the most common types of commercially available "10 Essentials," or survival products, and analyzed their usefulness for different types of situations. Where appropriate, I've recommended currently available models that have been fully vetted by me or one of my many gear testers. Shopping for this stuff can be overwhelming, and I hope I've helped you figure out what's right for you. I've also included many survival tips and tricks that will help get you out of tough situations. Every piece of gear in your pack has—or should have—multiple uses, if you just have a few tricks up your sleeve.

This is a tiny book! It was difficult to cram it all in, but you can find so much more information on all these topics—including reviews of the latest and greatest gear—at backpacker.com.

I'd like to thank several people who helped me with this book. Joe Flowers, a longtime *Backpacker* contributor and survival expert, provided excellent advice and many photos. My friend Kris Wagner, a navigation guru, helped me hone the navigation chapter with tons of no-nonsense advice. And my buddies Ben Fullerton and Andrew Bydlon, *Backpacker*'s ace photographers, generously provided me with lots of gorgeous images. Thanks, guys!

Chapter One

Shelter

Home, sweet home. It's amazing how much comfort and protection a little nylon dome can provide, even in the harshest conditions. Adequate shelter is arguably the most butt-saving essential (especially in bad weather), whether you're headed off on a multiday trip or find yourself in a survival situation. I've been on trips when the rain was so bad that we were forced to spend days confined within the thin walls of a little tent. At times like that, you begin to understand the wisdom of buying a tent with a little extra elbowroom and a vestibule big enough to let you cook in.

TENTS

They come in a dizzying array of shapes, sizes, configurations, and materials. Some key questions to ask yourself when shopping for a tent:

1. What season(s) will I use it in? Summer tents are all or mostly mesh (for maximum ventilation), with a waterproof fly for rainy nights. Three-season tents are the most versatile, incorporating a combo of mesh and nylon walls, a full-coverage rainfly, and

a stronger pole structure that can hold up to hard winds and a few inches of surprise snowfall. Mountain or four-season tents have more rigid pole structures and more weatherproofing (you won't find unprotected mesh).

2. What size do I need? You'll have to decide whether you want a solo tent, a two-person, a three-person, etc. But even within those ranges, tents can vary a ton in terms of interior space. And remember: Weight increases with volume. Crawl into your top candidates—with your partner(s) and gear—to get a clear sense of living space, including headroom, elbowroom, and length. Also pay attention to vestibule space. Some tents offer huge exterior storage and cooking space, while others offer little more than a portico for a few pairs of boots. Snow-campers and people who live in or travel to particularly wet climates, such as the Pacific Northwest, need extra tent space—for accommodating extra gear, dressing inside the tent, and preparing meals inside the vestibule. But if you're a fair-weather-only camper, consider downsizing. If you're only sleeping in the tent,

you don't need the extra space and weight (see below).

3. What are my weight parameters? You'll need to think hard about your tolerance for carrying the load versus your need for living space. Bigger, stronger tents will obviously weigh more, but don't be tempted to buy more tent than you'll actually need. Freestanding tents (they require few or no poles to stand fully erected) generally weigh a little more but offer more staking/pitching convenience; non-freestanding tents require careful staking and a surface that's hospitable to staking (this can be tricky in sand, rocky soil, snow, and on rock). Shaped tarps are the lightest-weight option and, when properly rigged, can provide surprising shelter from bad weather (but no bug protection).

Tip: For much more information about choosing a tent, plus all the latest product reviews, go to backpacker.com.

EMERGENCY SHELTERS

Even on day hikes, it's wise to pack some sort of "survival shelter." They typically weigh only a few ounces and pack down to the size of a sandwich, and if the stuff hits the fan and you find yourself stuck out there, they're lifesavers. There's no shortage of products out there that are marketed as "survival shelters." Be sure to get one with a silvery coating on at least one side so that you have the option of using it as a heat reflector. And remember: No matter what the packaging says, you will not be warm and cozy in or under these things. The reality is that you'll have an utterly miserable night, but you will make it through

These survival shelters can be rigged in numerous ways to help stave off hypothermia. Clockwise from left: Adventure Medical Kits Sport Utility Blanket, Heatsheets Emergency Bivvy, Coghlan's Emergency Blanket. *Kristin Hostetter*

till morning. Here's a rundown of the most common types of commercially available products:

Space blanket. These thin Mylar sheets are cheap (under $5), ultralight, and ultrapackable, but they're fragile, generally small, very loud and crinkly, and often only good for one use. Example: Coghlan's Emergency Blanket

Emergency bivvy. Thin, stretchy polyethylene body sacks have taped seams and a heat-reflective inner coating. They are generally more protective (for one person), more durable, and reusable and can boost the warmth of a sleeping bag by up to 15ºF. But they're slightly heavier and bulkier, more expensive (up to $20), and less versatile for augmenting built shelters. Example: Adventure Medical Kits Heatsheets Emergency Bivvy

Multipurpose emergency blanket. These often look like Mylar blankets but are much thicker and more durable, made of a woven, ripstop material. Although heavier and bulkier than the above options, they'll last way longer and often include corner grommets to help with rigging. Example: Adventure Medical Kits Sport Utility Blanket

Plastic sheeting. Clear plastic fabric found at any home improvement store can be cut to any size. It's rugged, cheap, and can help fortify any self-built shelter from rain and wind.

Double Duty

If you need more incentive to carry some sort of shelter material, here you go. Any of the emergency shelters listed above can be used in myriad ways to help a survivor. Think outside the box!

>> Collect or hold water.
>> Place silvery side face up to attract rescue.
>> Reflect heat from a fire.
>> Use as a ground cloth.
>> Use as a waterproof gear cover.
>> Carry firewood.
>> Augment/fortify a natural-materials shelter (see "Making Do: Shelter Building").

MAKING DO: SHELTER BUILDING

Let's say you're on a day hike. You have every intention of being home before dark, so you've shunned the rules and neglected to pack a shelter or anything in the way of warm clothes either. You get lost, bad weather rolls in, and nighttime descends. You realize that you won't be sleeping in a bed tonight. Bummer.

Some basic shelter-building skills should be part of every hiker's repertoire. There are dozens of different types of shelters you can make, ranging from elaborate to spartan. But in most cases, all you want to do is make it through the night safely, so let's focus on the spartan. Plus, getting a fire going, and gathering enough fuel to keep it going through the night, is generally a more valuable use of your time and energy than building a fancy shelter.

The first thing you need to do is locate the best spot. If you're above treeline, go down. There's simply more protection and shelter-building resources in the forest. Look for some natural protection—under a thick canopy or a rocky outcropping, against a big boulder (to block wind and reflect heat), or under a big downed tree.

Lean-to

A lean-to is the quickest, easiest shelter to make and can range from super simple to quite bomber. You could build a small lean-to using an emergency blanket (pictured), but it won't offer much protection. A far better solution: Build it using natural materials,

If time is short and you need shelter fast, rig a lean-to using tarp material. If it has a reflective side, like this one, make sure it's facing down toward you so it can reflect your own body heat back at you, as well as any heat created by a fire built in front of it. *Joe Flowers*

and use your space blanket either as a heat-reflective liner or a bottom sheet. The best lean-tos consist of a sturdy ridgepole (secure it between two trees or with self-constructed stick tripods). Lay a series of sticks from the ridgepole angling down to the ground, then cover the sticks with a thick layer of dry leaves, branches, pine boughs, etc. Add small sidewalls for more protection. The cool thing about a lean-to is that you can build a fire right in front, line the inside wall with your reflective blanket, and feel the heat bounce at you from two directions.

Debris Hut

Debris huts work best in cold situations, when sustaining a fire all night long isn't an option. It can take more than several hours to build a good one, but

Debris huts are very effective at providing shelter and require little more than time and what you find in the forest. *Joe Flowers*

once finished, the thick walls of leafy insulation can keep you warm in well below freezing temperatures. The basic idea is to build an A-frame structure with a long ridgepole that you situate about crotch high at the head end, tapering down to foot height. Place ribs (sticks) all along the ridgepole, and then pile it high with dry debris such as leaves and pine boughs. Walls should be at least 2 feet thick. Drag more dry debris inside the shelter to provide bottom insulation and to fill any empty space inside the cavity.

Building a Snow Shelter

The fastest, easiest type of snow shelter is a quinzhee. Basically, you make a huge pile of snow and then methodically hollow it out from the inside. It's fun to practice in the yard with your kids after a big storm. Some key points:

» Take it slow so that you don't work up a sweat. In frigid temps, hypothermia can be right on the heels of sweat.

» Let your snow pile set for 20 to 60 minutes before digging into it.

» Keep the walls at least 5 or 6 inches thick to avoid collapse.

» Poke an air vent through the top to prevent carbon monoxide buildup.

» Pile excavated snow into walls on either side of the door to block wind.

» Use your emergency blanket as a ground cloth.

Makeshift Grommets

Trying to rig a tarp with no grommets in the corners? No problem. Find a small pebble—about the size of a grape—and push it into the underside of your tarp to form a small pocket; then tie your cord tightly around the stone. **Note:** Whatever you do, don't poke holes in your tarp material—it will only lead to tears.

Use this rigging technique on any material that lacks reinforced grommets in the corners. It's sturdy and doesn't require you to cut your material. All you need is a small pebble and some cordage. *Kristin Hostetter*

Know This Knot: Tautline Hitch

Practice this until it becomes second nature. Because when it's dark and cold and you're scared, fumbling around with knots you haven't practiced since Cub Scouts is no fun. The tautline hitch is a sliding knot that's ideal for rigging tarps; once it's affixed to an anchor point (say, a rock that you're using to secure your tarp), you can easily adjust the tautness.

Start by wrapping the line around your fixed anchor point. Make three turns (toward your anchor) around the standing part of the line.

Bring the working end toward you, and make a half hitch in front of the first turn.

Pull to tighten.

Clyde Soles

Chapter Two

Fire

There's nothing like a good campfire, right? In the best of circumstances, a campfire is the hearth and home of a campsite: the place where stories unfold, marshmallows are toasted, and memories are made. But fires are much more than that. The ability to make a fire in any conditions can help the survivalist on many fronts. Of course warmth is the big one, but there are lots of other benefits to fire: It can be used to signal for help, dry out soaked gear, provide light, boil water, cook food, and deter animals and mosquitoes. And perhaps most important, a fire can make you feel better—safer, less alone, more hopeful, and more optimistic.

Many people don't feel they've camped out unless they spend an evening sitting by a fire. ©Maga/licensed by Shutterstock.com

Reality check: Making a sustainable fire in a real-world survival situation is bloody hard. When you need fire the most—in cold, wet conditions—it's hardest to create. You likely have frigid, stiff fingers, nothing but wet wood and tinder around you, fading light, deteriorating weather, and so much adrenaline pumping through your body that you might feel dizzy, out of breath, or panicky.

That's why the focus of this chapter is on foolproof fire-making and ensuring you have all the right tools to get it crackling. Forget about making a friction fire. It looks really cool on all the survival shows, but what you don't see is the hours and the buckets of sweat lost in the process. It's practically impossible, and you'll spend so much time and energy attempting it that you won't have anything leftover for, well, anything else.

FIRE-STARTING GEAR

The good news is that fire-starting gear is practically weightless, yet it can save your bacon in a dire situation. On every trip, always pack at least two—preferably three—methods of creating fire. A disposable lighter is an absolute must. Make sure it works and has plenty of fuel. For your second source, you've got several choices:

Waterproof matches. The best ones are dipped in wax or some other material to make them burn

Fire-starting gear takes many shapes. Pack at least two methods of creating a flame (preferably three). Clockwise from top left: UCO Stormproof Match Kit, Coghlan's Magnesium Fire Starter, Bic lighter, County Comm Peanut Lighter, Soto Pocket Torch, Light My Fire Swedish FireSteel 2.0, Spyderco Manix2 steel knife. *Kristin Hostetter*

longer and come in a watertight case with a striking surface. Recommended: UCO Stormproof Match Kit (industrialrev.com)

Magnesium block. Magnesium takes a spark very easily but can be tricky to use, because in real-world conditions, those tiny shavings tend to blow around. You must shave the spine of the magnesium block until you have a small pile (nickel-size, at least) of material nestled into your dry tinder; then hit it with a spark (from flint or a ferro rod). Recommended: Coghlan's Magnesium Fire Starter (coghlans.com)

Bic lighter.

Peanut lighter. These refillable lighters are—you guessed it—peanut-size, and thanks to a rubber

O-ring around the cap, totally waterproof. Despite the lighter's diminutive size, the lighter fluid seems to last forever. Recommended: County Comm Peanut Lighter (countycomm.com)

Flint. Flint is a hard sedimentary rock found in nature. When struck with steel, it will throw a spark. But the flint sparks have a relatively low temperature, so it's tough to ignite anything but char cloth (see page 24).

Steel or carbon steel knife. Use your blade to create a spark with ferro or flint. *Tip:* Always use the thicker, blunt back of the blade for sparking so that it doesn't wear down your cutting edge.

Ferro rod. Also known as ferrocerium, fire steel, misch metal, or metal matches, a ferro rod is a man-made, pencil-thin stick of hardened rare earth metals and iron. It's the stuff used in cigarette lighters. When scraped with steel (like your knife blade), it showers tons of tiny hot sparks onto a well-prepared tinder pile and produces fire. Ferro rods are often mistakenly called "flint" (see above), but they differ from flint in that they are man-made and generally a bit easier to use than a natural flint. Recommended: Light My Fire Swedish FireSteel 2.0 (lightmyfire.com)

Torch lighter. Like mini blowtorches, these devices produce a hot, directed flame that makes fire-starting easy. Recommended: Soto Pocket Torch (sotooutdoors.com)

How to Dry a Wet Bic

If your lighter takes a swim and stops working and you don't have the time or patience to wait for it to dry (it will, eventually), use this technique to get it back in business right away: Pop off the smooth center section of the striker wheel with the tip of your knife. This exposes the inner workings of the striker. Use a piece of gauze (or any absorbent material) from your first-aid kit to wipe down the wheel, removing any carbon buildup that may be holding water. Rotate the wheel until all sides are clean and all moisture is absorbed, and flick.

MAKING DO: SURVIVAL FIRES

This section is all about making a fire the hard way—with tools (aka fire steels) rather than a lighter or matches. Don't expect that you'll be able to do this in the heat of the moment if you've never practiced it. Fire-making is a skill that you should practice every chance you get, even at home in the fireplace. Challenge yourself to make "one-match fires." Scavenge materials from your yard and prepare them in your fireplace. Pretend you're in the woods with only one match. Can you get it cranking? If you can't do it at home in the comfort of your living room, you're guaranteed to have trouble out in the wilds, so keep practicing.

For a successful fire you need four things: tinder (dry, fluffy, fine material formed into a bird's-nest shape), kindling (small, toothpick to pencil-size sticks), fuel (larger logs that will sustain the fire), and of course your spark or flame. Before you begin, gather all your materials into three neat piles, which will make nurturing your fire easier. The key here is to find dry stuff, which can be tricky if it has been raining.

Finding Materials

Two words: *fluffy* and *dry*. It sounds simple, but it can be tough to find the good stuff when you're stuck in the damp woods or high on a blustery mountain. Keep your eyes peeled for the low-hanging fruit: cattails, abandoned bird's nests, pine needles, dead grasses. All these things can catch a spark from a fire steel. (I'm not saying it's easy, just doable!) Look under big downed logs, under overhangs, or under thick canopies.

A fluffy, dry tinder bundle is your first step in making a fire.
Joe Flowers

Can't find anything? Look for a dead stick, preferably upright or stuck in a tree snag—in other words, not sitting on the wet ground. Use your knife to make fine shavings, collecting them in a hat or pot or jacket. After the first few passes, aim your knife for the corners of your last cut to shave off finer pieces, using a slicing and pushing motion simultaneously.

Ignition

It's pretty simple: To make fire you need a flame or a spark. Easy, if you have a working lighter (which you

Stack kindling in a tepee formation, beginning with small, pencil-size sticks and building outward to larger ones. Be sure to leave lots of room between the sticks so the fire can breathe.
©Jason Patrick Ross/licensed by Shutterstock.com

should always pack), but what if you lose it? Break out your backup spark-throwing device (see pages 15–17). Make sure your tinder bundle is protected from wind on all sides. Nothing sucks more than getting your tinder to catch, only to have it blow away in a big gust. If it's raining, make a mini-lean-to of dry kindling as a roof to protect the tinder while you're working.

Once your tinder bundle is burning, quickly add your smallest sticks and twigs to the flame (no bigger than pencil-size at first), taking care not to smother it. Maintaining good airflow in your infant fire is key. The tepee method works well. Keep adding sticks; as the fire grows, you can add bigger and bigger ones. *Tip:* The more time you invest in prepping your materials, the more successful your fire-starting efforts will be.

Maintenance

Fires like to breathe, and they like extra oxygen. As you build your infant fire, take care not to smother it; leave plenty of spaces between the little stuff. Think about how flames rise, and try to build a vertical structure that will light from below. Blowing on a fire can help it grow. Long, controlled breaths will get the fire hotter than short, powerful bursts. *Tip:* Use a straw or metal pipe, such as a tent pole section, to concentrate the airstream.

Feather Sticks

Also known as fuzz sticks, these are great sources of kindling. The idea is to take a medium-size piece of kindling and use your knife to create more surface area, which helps the stick ignite. Here are some tips on how to make a feather stick (practice at home!):

» A very sharp fixed-blade knife works best for this task. But any type of knife will do, as long

When making feather or fuzz sticks, the key is to cut the smallest, thinnest of slivers—and lots of them! *Joe Flowers*

as you can get a comfortable, safe grip on the handle.

» Start with a stick that's about 1 inch in diameter and about 18 inches long. Rest one end on a stable, flat surface, such as a rock. Using steady pressure, begin shaving long, thin curls down the stick.

» Rotate the stick regularly to utilize the edges of the previous cut.

» Keep the knife blade at a shallow angle so the shavings stay as thin as possible.

» Don't worry if some of the tendrils fall off. Save them, and use them in the fire.

How to Make Char Cloth

Char cloth is simply cotton fabric that's been heated in a sealed metal container until it blackens. When it's hit with any spark, the fabric begins to smolder and can then be used to coax a fire out of dry tinder. Make a batch of char cloth at home, carry it in a tiny ziplock baggie (it weighs next to nothing), and you'll always have a fire at your fingertips.

To make char cloth, you'll need a camp stove, some squares of cotton, and an airtight tin with a hole punched in the lid. Also shown is a small plastic bag for sealing completed char cloth. *Kristin Hostetter*

Within a few seconds of ignition, smoke will billow out from the hole. When the smoke stops, remove the canister from the heat and let cool. *Kristin Hostetter*

This is what completed char cloth looks like. *Kristin Hostetter*

Step 1: Cut 3 x 3-inch squares from an old cotton T-shirt.

Step 2: Find a small airtight metal container—an Altoid or shoe polish tin works well, or you can buy a small empty paint container at the hardware store. Use an awl or nail to poke a hole in the center of the lid.

Step 3: Place three or four squares of cotton in the container and place it on a canister stove set on low. (Do this outside, because it generates a lot of smoke.) Cook the cloth for a minute or two. Smoke will billow out of the hole; when the smoke stops, remove the canister from the heat and let it cool completely before removing your char cloth.

Chapter Three
Extra Clothing

Few things in my pack are dearer to me than my warm jacket. Even if I don't need it, I love knowing that it's there for me. And at the end of a day, or on the top of a gusty peak, there's nothing like slipping into a cocoon of warmth.

Packing a little extra clothing on any wilderness trip is a smart plan. I'm not suggesting that you pack a fresh shirt or undies for every day of the week. In fact, I've been known to wear the same shirt for six days straight and rotate between two pairs of socks for eight days. But you need to have the right system of clothing with you at all times to make sure you can withstand any weather that hits.

There's no need to pack the whole closet—just the right combination of layers you can mix and match to stay comfortable and safe in any conditions. *Fullerton Images*

The first thing everyone does when reaching camp is slip into his or her big, warm puffy jacket. *Kristin Hostetter*

WHAT TO PACK FOR DAY HIKES

Of course you'll look at the forecast and dress for the day: shorts or long pants, a short-sleeve or long-sleeve T-shirt, a light jacket or a warmer one. Always toss a light rain shell in the bottom of your pack. It will not only keep you dry if a surprise storm rolls in but also will cut the wind and provide you with some warmth if you need it.

WHAT TO PACK AND WEAR ON MULTIDAY TRIPS

First, get used to your own smell. It might drive you crazy for the first day or so, but after a few days in the wild, you'll get used to it, I promise. And if you pack the right fabrics (see "Avoid Cotton"), you can keep stink to a minimum. Here's a look at what clothes to pack for multiday trips.

Warm Weather

- » technical (non-cotton) T-shirt
- » long-sleeve shirt
- » shorts
- » long pants (Save some pack space and weight by getting a pair of zip-off convertible pants.)
- » warm jacket (fleece, down, or synthetic puffy)
- » rain shell
- » rain pants
- » socks (two pairs for trips up to a week; a third pair for longer trips)
- » undies (whatever minimum you feel comfortable with)
- » sun hat

Cold Weather

- » long-sleeve base layer
- » long john bottoms
- » soft-shell pants
- » warm midlayer (fleece, or thin down or synthetic puffy)
- » camp coat (big, puffy, warm down or synthetic jacket with hood)
- » hard-shell jacket (with hood)
- » hard-shell pants
- » socks (two pairs for trips up to a week; a third pair for longer trips)
- » undies (whatever minimum you feel comfortable with)

- » warm hat
- » light gloves (for walking)
- » warm gloves/mittens (for in camp)
- » neck gaiter

Avoid Cotton

It's great for everyday use, but aside from really dry, sunny environments (like the desert), cotton is a liability in the backcountry for several reasons:

1. Once wet, cotton takes forever to dry unless you have strong bright sun. So when you sweat through your T-shirt on a big climb, your pack straps may start to chafe where the cotton stays wet underneath. The same goes for cotton socks.
2. Cotton loses its shape over multiple days, so a T-shirt that started off fitting you well will likely be stretched out and flapping after a few sweat-and-cool cycles.
3. If you need a little extra warmth, cotton doesn't provide it.
4. Cotton is not as durable and tear resistant as other outdoor fabrics.

Bottom line: There are far better fabrics to choose from. Synthetic fabrics (polyesters and nylons) dry in a snap and are very strong for their weight. Polyester shirts wick sweat extremely well, and they don't lose their shape over time. However, synthetic fabrics (especially polyester) tend to get stinky pretty quickly. Wool is another fabric to consider. Today's wool is super-fine and soft. It resists odor even after days of use, and it can be toasty warm but still breathable. Wools typically don't dry quite as fast, though, so sweat hogs tend to prefer synthetics.

LAYERING 101

Staying comfortable in the outdoors is all about layering. The key is to have a system of clothing that you can use in different combinations to stay warm and dry. A basic layering system consists of three parts:

Base layer. Your next-to-skin layer is responsible for wicking sweat away from your body when you're working hard. As discussed above ("Avoid Cotton"), synthetics and wool are your best option here, as they will wick sweat, dry quickly, and help you maintain a consistent body temperature.

Mid layer. This is your insulating layer. Depending on the season and location of your trip, you might choose

Your next-to-skin layer has a big job: Wick sweat quickly away from your skin and dry fast, even while you're working hard. Your mid and outer layers will vary depending on the weather conditions. *Fullerton Images*

a very thin fleece, a light wool jacket or sweater, or a puffy insulated jacket (again, avoid cotton; it doesn't insulate well). As for puffies, you have many different types of insulation to choose from: Synthetic fills (like PrimaLoft) are generally less expensive, and they are virtually impossible to get wet because synthetic fills don't absorb water. If a synthetic jacket does get wet, just put it on. Your body heat will dry it in a matter of minutes, and the jacket will keep you warm in the process. Down is the lightest, warmest fill you can buy. It's more expensive, but it packs down extremely well, whereas synthetic fills are generally bulkier to pack. But down—even the new variations, which have been treated for water-resistance—will eventually get wet and lose their loft. When they do, they lose their ability to insulate, and they dry slower than synthetics. Treated down will dry a little faster (and with fewer clumps), but the bottom line is that you want to steer clear of soakings if you're wearing down.

Shell. Your outer layer has two jobs: Cut the wind, and repel precipitation. Look for a hooded hard-shell fabric made of a waterproof/breathable fabric such as Gore-Tex, eVent, or Pertex Shield. Make sure your shell jacket is roomy enough to accommodate all your other layers underneath. If you're a heavy sweater, consider getting one with pit zips (venting zippers underneath the arms).

Survival Smarts: Drying Wet Clothes

When you only have a limited supply of things to wear and they get wet—either from rain, sweat, or an unintended fall into the drink—you need a few tricks up your sleeve for getting them dry fast. The best thing you can do—barring ample sunshine and time—is continue to wear them, as unappealing as that might sound. Keep wet clothes on, and wear your shell gear on top. Your own body heat is you best chance at getting them dry. At night, wear the wet clothes inside your sleeping bag, or lay them out flat against your body. Avoid balling them up at the foot of your sleeping bag or trying to line dry them in your tent. If you do, chances are they'll be just as wet in the morning—and miserably cold to put on again.

Chapter Four

Hydration

You can live only up to five days without water, so if you're in trouble, make finding water a priority. Even if you're not in trouble, staying hydrated should always be at the forefront of your mind. Hikers should drink between three and five quarts per day, depending on the temperature, the altitude, and your level of exertion. All backcountry water should be treated in some fashion (with chemicals, a filtering device, or by boiling), but if you don't have the means to treat your water, drink anyway. You're more likely to die of dehydration than you are of a stomach bug (which will likely hit long after you get home, anyway).

When possible, treat all backcountry water before drinking. If treating is not possible, drink anyway.
Fullerton Images

THE GEAR

At the bare minimum, always have a water bottle with you, even on the shortest of hikes. Bottles are tough to improvise (unless you find someone else's garbage), and the importance of staying hydrated cannot be overstated.

Bottle. It doesn't matter what type you bring, as long as you bring something. Even a convenience store bottle that once held Evian will last for a long time with care. Gatorade bottles (32-ounce) are among the lightest you can get, and they're sturdy enough to last for an entire season (or more).

Pot. If you're on a multiday trip, you probably have some sort of metal cook pot in your pack, which is a critical instrument for collecting and treating water (as well as countless other tasks).

Clockwise from top left: cook pot, Platypus GravityWorks, SteriPen Freedom, Aquamira Frontier Filter, Nalgene Wide-Mouth Bottle, Sawyer Squeeze Filter, MSR HyperFlow, Aquamira Water Treatment Drops. *Kristin Hostetter*

Ziplock plastic bag (1-gallon size). These are useful for holding water and making water through transpiration (see below). They weigh nothing, so always pack one or two.

Chemical tablets or drops. These ultralight tablets or drops will turn even the nastiest water potable. But they won't change the taste or appearance of gross water, and they take from 30 minutes up to 3 hours to work properly. Recommended: MSR Aquatabs (cascadedesigns.com) or Aquamira Water Treatment Drops (aquamira.com)

Pump filters. Like the other two types of filters mentioned below, pumps reliably remove sediment and pathogens. Your muscle power creates the suction that pulls the water through an intake hose, pushes it through the filter element, and spits it out clean on the other side. Pump filters are usually the heaviest and bulkiest treatment method, and they require some maintenance to prevent clogging. If you pack a filter, be sure you know how to maintain it in the field (see "Filter TLC"). Recommended: MSR HyperFlow (cascadedesigns.com)

Bottle filters. These handy units are a snap to use. Just unscrew the top, dip the bottle in the water, replace the cap, and suck or squeeze (depending on the model) the water through an integrated filter element inside. They're fairly light and compact, but the filters themselves tend to clog more often than pump filters making suction difficult, and diligent cleaning is a must. Recommended: Sawyer Squeeze Water Filter (sawyer.com)

Straw filters. These affordable, ultralight slurpers are great to pack as a backup. They are essentially just straws with integrated in-line filters, ideal for sucking water from shallow puddles in places where water is scarce. You just lie down on your belly next to a puddle or stream, place one end of the straw in the water, and suck. You won't get copious amounts, but you will get enough to keep you going. Recommended: Aquamira Frontier Filter (aquamira.com)

Gravity filters. Ideal for large groups working from a base camp, gravity filters consist of two bladders connected by a hose with an in-line filter. Just hang a bag of untreated water from a tree, and let gravity do its thing. Water will drip through the filter into the "clean" bag while you perform other chores. Recommended: Platypus GravityWorks (cascadedesigns.com)

UV wands. Light, packable, and super fast, UV devices rely on battery power and UV rays to neutralize pathogens. Just dip the wand in the water, press a button, swirl for about 90 seconds, and guzzle away. UV treatments don't work well in murky water with lots of sediment (let water sit for 30 minutes or so before treating). And be sure to pack a wide-mouth bottle that's compatible with the wand. Recommended: SteriPen Freedom (steripen.com)

FILTER TLC

Here are a few tricks for keeping your filter working properly in the field.

If you have a ceramic filter element, which are known for their durability and longevity (as well as their hefty weight), you can remove the filter element and scrub it with one of those green kitchen scrubby sponges to remove any sediment that has built up on the outer surface. Once a year or so, sterilize the filter by dropping it into a pot of boiling water for about 5 minutes. (**Note:** Check your owner's manual before doing this; some companies do not recommend it. And be sure to remove any O-rings around the filter, which can get deformed and damaged by high heat.)

Glass-fiber filters rely on an intricate network of folds—and the vast surface area they provide—to trap micro-cooties. When your glass-fiber filter becomes difficult to pump, remove the element and swish it aggressively in clean water to release any sediment caught in the folds.

Most filters can also be **backflushed** when you start to notice pumping resistance. Backflushing is easy and quick; it entails running the water backwards through the filter to free any built-up gunk. Check your owner's manual to learn how to back-flush your particular device.

The Boil Method

Long before fancy filters or UV-zappers were invented, boiling was the only foolproof water treatment method, and it still works just as well today. Heating water to boiling obliterates anything living in your water, but the method does have some drawbacks. You need a stove (with plenty of fuel) or a good hot fire and a vessel to contain the water. Plus, you need patience. It can take up to 10 minutes to boil water (depending on the heat source and the conditions), and then you need to let it cool—unless you want to parboil your tongue.

MAKING DO

Finding Water

Streams, rivers, lakes, ponds, and puddles are obvious. But sometimes water is scarce, so you have to know where to look for it.

- » Look in valleys or low areas where water will naturally drain.
- » Locate lush, green foliage; water is generally nearby.
- » Check rock crevices and caves where rainwater may have collected.
- » Keep your eyes out for muddy, damp ground (then follow the "Make Water from a Sock" tip, page 40).

Filtering Smarts

Follow these tips to get the best results with any filtering device.

» Look for calm, clear pools. To preserve the life of your filter, avoid pumping or gathering water from roiling rivers where sediment is flowing.

» Let water settle. If you're forced to use sediment-infused water, let it settle in a big pot or waterproof stuff sack before filtering.

» Adjust the intake hose float. Pump filters have little buoys on the end of the intake hose. Adjust yours so that the intake pre-filter floats in the water rather than resting on the bottom, where it will suck debris into the filter and clog it.

» Don't overuse it. There's no need to filter water you'll be boiling for dinner. Boiling is a foolproof sterilizer.

» Keep it cozy. In cold weather, water inside the filter element can freeze up, making pumping difficult or impossible. Wrap your filter in a ziplock bag and tuck it into your sleeping bag on cold nights.

» Be gentle. Big drops or sharp impact can damage the filter element (especially ceramic), so don't be clumsy, and be sure to pack it in a protected place inside your pack.

» Watch for animal tracks, especially where they converge. Animals always know the local watering holes.

» Look for swarming insects, which usually indicate a nearby water source.

» Watch the skies. Birds often circle above water.

Make Water from a Sock

Bear Grylls taught me this one (seriously!). If you find yourself in a mucky situation—surrounded by lots of wet clay, dirt, or mud but no water holes—fill your sock with wet glop, then squeeze until water makes its way through the fibers—either directly into your mouth or a vessel. Gross? You bet. But it's better than dying of dehydration.

Straining water through your sock may be a last-ditch, desperate measure and the water may taste like a combo of smelly feet and dirt, but it could save your butt if you really need water.
Fullerton Images

Make a Transpiration Solar Still

If you have access to any sort of green vegetation, a plastic bag, and a tiny bit of cordage, you can create water. I find this method simpler and more foolproof than a ground-based solar still. Just place the bag over live vegetation in a sunny spot, put a pebble in the bag to create a low spot in which water can settle, tie it off at the top, and wait. The sun heats the bag and draws moisture from the vegetation, which

Transpiration still tip: Place a small (clean) pebble in one corner of the bag. It will weight it, creating a low point where water will collect. *Kristin Hostetter*

collects at the lowest point of the bag. Depending on the sun and the temperature, you can collect up to several cups per day.

Tip: Use the largest clear (not black) bags you can find, and encase as much vegetation as you can in the bag. Pick a spot that will get full sun all day. If you have multiple bags, make multiple stills.

Survival Smarts: Water Collection

When rain rolls in, gather water in any and all vessels you have: extra tarp material, rain jackets and pants, plastic baggies, stuff sacks, etc. Anything that holds water should be repurposed as a rain-catcher. Place bottles and pots near the low corners of an erected tarp to siphon off drippage.

Chapter Five
Food

Food is gear, right? It's certainly a key part of any hiking trip. I plan my food for any trip pretty meticulously, but I always have some extra just in case I get stuck out there for longer than I expected. (It's happened to me before; I remember digging through my garbage bag once in Isle Royal National Park to scoop out used coffee grinds!) When it comes to food for hiking and backpacking, there are three main things to consider: nutritional content, packability/perishability, and weight. As for taste? It goes without saying. There's no reason your trail food shouldn't be yummy.

Fuel your adventures with hearty, tasty, nourishing meals like this easy-to-make penne with veggies and cheese.
Andrew Bydlon

NUTRITION

To perform at your best and be your strongest, pay attention to the ratio of the types of food you eat.

Complex carbohydrates. Fifty percent of a hiker's food should be complex carbs. Fiber-rich foods like whole-grain pasta, brown rice, oatmeal, and whole wheat crackers or bread slowly break down in your stomach and give you sustained energy all day long.

Fat. Go for a 30 percent ratio of good, unsaturated fats, like those found in nuts and fish. Cheese is also a good source of fat (although the saturated kind). I can't imagine a hiking trip without a big hunk of cheddar. Aside from providing calories and fat, it just makes everything taste better.

Protein. Aim for about a 20 percent ratio of protein (preferably lean). You can find protein in beans, jerky, salami, almonds, cheese, and vacuum-sealed wild salmon.

Simple sugars. Popping a couple hard candies or chowing down on a Snickers bar is a great way to give yourself a burst of quick energy to get you up a steep climb. But you'll crash soon, so be sure to have some more sustainable energy foods at the ready.

Salt. Most hikers don't have to worry too much about salt intake, because we lose lots of salt through sweat. Salty snacks like pretzels and jerky will replace your body's needs, and most pre-packaged backpacking meals are fairly heavily salted, so you rarely need to add more to make them palatable.

Counting Calories

Hiking is hard work, especially when it entails carrying a big backpack and rigorous terrain. Here's what you can expect to burn out there.

Average Man

Relaxing in camp	2,400–2,600 calories
Day hiking	+515 calories per hour
Backpacking	+620 calories per hour (more for high altitudes)
Cold weather backpacking	+680–740 calories per hour

Average Woman

Relaxing in camp	1,800–2,000 calories
Day hiking	+410 calories per hour
Backpacking	+490 calories per hour (more for high altitudes)
Cold weather backpacking	+540–590 calories per hour

Survival Smarts: Foraging

If you find yourself stuck out there with nothing to eat, resist the urge to start foraging, unless you have a firm grasp on what's safe and what's not. You can survive for a good long time without food. (Ghandi fasted for twenty-one days when he was in his 70s!) It won't be fun, and you'll have to learn to ignore the incessant rumble in your stomach, but as long as you have water, you'll be able to survive long enough to make it safely home.

PACKABILITY AND PERISHABILITY

Day hikers have no limit to what they can bring. Pack sushi in an insulated container, a crunchy salad with grilled chicken in a lidded plastic bowl. I even know people who stop at Burger King for bacon double cheeseburgers before a hike.

But backpackers need to think about what items will survive the rigors of the trail. Meats (if precooked or frozen) can last up to a day or two, and some fruits and veggies can last up to a few days. But for the most part, we rely on dry, shelf-staple ingredients. Here are a few fresh items that travel really well and are great to pack on longer trips. They perk up any meal with big flavor and texture.

Pack fresh produce inside your cooking pot to keep it protected. *Kristin Hostetter*

- » Garlic: It lasts forever and is a huge flavor enhancer for any savory meal.
- » Onion: Ditto.
- » Fresh ginger: A small knob is practically weightless and adds incredible zing to any Asian dish.

- » Cheese: Hard cheeses like cheddar or Parmesan are mandatory for sandwiches, and they make great dinner toppers for everything from burritos to pasta to rice.
- » Peppers: Bell or jalapeño peppers stay firm for up to five days without refrigeration and add crunch to any savory dish.
- » Apples: Packed carefully, they'll go for more than a week. They're great for amping up your morning oatmeal or on a sandwich with cheddar.
- » Oranges: An orange on day four or five of a trip is the most amazing treat.

WEIGHT

Some of us are fanatical ounce-counters, others less so. Either way, food will be one of the heaviest items in your pack if you're not careful. Commercially available dehydrated meals have improved vastly over

Tuscan Beef Stew by Packit Gourmet (packitgourmet .com) is one of the tastiest prepackaged meals I've tried. It looks and tastes like something from home!
Jeff Mullins

the past few years, and if you're willing to pay for the convenience of having someone do all the prep and packing work, you can find delicious, satisfying meals that require only boiling water. Recommended: anything from Packit Gourmet (packitgourmet.com.)

If you'd rather come up with your own concoctions, invest in a dehydrator for around $50 (nesco .com). Suddenly, a whole new world of eating is open to you. You can precook and dehydrate pasta (so it cooks faster in camp); make dried banana, apple, and mango chips by the bucket; and dehydrate all your favorite ingredients, from hamburger to ground chicken, carrots to cabbage, peppers to peas. Then just mix and match your favorite ingredients and spices to create an endless array of meals.

Best of all, you can dehydrate your family favorites. Maybe it's your famous red pepper and Vidalia onion sauce. Or grandma's Bolognese. Or it could be that spicy salsa you make from homegrown veggies.

You'll save big bucks and be able to create countless healthy and delicious meals if you buy a dehydrator. Using one is time-intensive (all the prepping and chopping) but easy and worth it. Prepare large quantities at one time. Dehydrated food will keep for months in the refrigerator. ©elena moiseeva/licensed by Shutterstock.com

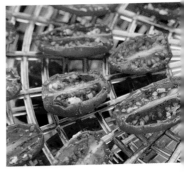

Whatever it is, you can probably dehydrate it. Real, homemade sauces, dips, and spreads taste just as good in the woods as they do at home, and they're easy to adapt. All you need are the plastic tray liners that work with your dehydrator. (You can also cut

Crowd Pleasers

These dinner recipes are two of my time-tested favorites. They're ideal for backpacking because they weigh only a few ounces per serving and require only boiling water to prepare.

Beef Stroganoff

Combine in a quart-size, freezer-weight ziplock baggie:

1 package beef-flavored Ramen (including seasoning packet)*

1/4 cup dehydrated ground beef

1/4 cup mixed dehydrated veggies

1 teaspoon paprika

Dash of cayenne pepper

Individual packet of cream cheese, equal to about a tablespoon (Grab one at your favorite bagel shop.)

Salt and pepper to taste

In camp add about 1 1/2 cups boiling water to baggie. Squish it around and let it rest in a cozy for about 10 minutes, or until the burger is tender. Stir in cream cheese.

*This recipe uses Ramen for quick prep times, but you can substitute cooked whole-grain pasta for more nutritional punch.

wax paper to fit, but be sure to lightly coat the paper with cooking spray so your sauce doesn't stick.) Spread the sauce in a thin layer and let it rip for 8 to 10 hours. The result is a featherweight leather that just requires hot water to reconstitute.

Spicy Curry Noodle Bowl

Combine in a quart-size, freezer-weight ziplock baggie:

1 serving of Asian cellophane noodles (They typically come in large bricks; break off a 3 × 6-inch chunk.)

Optional: 1/4 cup dehydrated meat of your choice (burger or chicken)

1/4 cup dehydrated mixed veggies

1 tablespoon curry

1 tablespoon cumin

1 tablespoon coriander

1 tablespoon garam masala

1/2 teaspoon ground ginger

2 tablespoons coconut cream powder

2 tablespoons dry milk

Dash of cayenne

Salt and pepper to taste

Handful of cashews (packed in a separate baggie)

In camp, add about 1 1/2 cups boiling water to baggie. Squish it around and let it rest in a cozy for about 10 minutes, or until everything is tender. Top with cashews.

SNACKING

Eating small bites throughout the day is key to maintaining energy and strength. Regular snacking can prevent bonking (when your gas tank suddenly goes dry and you find yourself completely exhausted), give you a quick burst of energy, and help you recover from a grueling day. Keep a snack or two handy and accessible while you hike. I like to stash a bar or small bag of trail mix in my pack's hip-belt pocket. The list of potential snacks is endless, but here are some of my faves:

My favorite trail snacks, from top: Honey Stinger Energy Chews, Clif Kit's Organic Fruit and Nut Bars, Sweetwood Jerky, home-made trail mix (aka gorp). *Kristin Hostetter*

Bars. Available in a mountain of brands and flavors, bars are a convenient, easy, and, in many cases, nutritionally dense. Grab a handful at the grocery store and taste-test them at home to find your favorites. Recommended: Clif Kit's Organic Fruit and Nut Bars (clifbar.com)

Gorp. Traditionally it stands for "good old raisins and peanuts," but gorp can be so much more. Buy it in bulk, or make your own using different dried fruits and nuts, plus M&M's (a must!), other candies, or other salty snacks like pretzel bits or Goldfish crackers.

Jerky. It's always a salty, satisfying crowd-pleaser. Plus, you can rehydrate it and mix it in with rice and veggies and spices for a hearty dinner. Recommended: Sweetwood Jerky (sweetwoodjerky.com)

Energy gels. These are great to pop like candy at the base of a hard climb or any time you need a quick burst of energy but don't have time to stop for a snack break. Recommended: Honey Stinger Energy Chews (honeystinger.com)

Survival Smarts: A Silver Lining

That wrapper on your energy bar can be repurposed into a signaling device, as long as it has a silvery lining, like so many do. Polish it with a little spit and flap it around like crazy in the sunlight to attract attention up to 1.5 miles away.

10 Killer Backpacking Foods	
Food	**Why**
almonds	High in good fats, protein, and fiber
sun-dried tomatoes	12 times more nutritional than regular tomatoes, high in vitamin C and iron; makes a great mix-in for any noodle, rice, or couscous dish
olive oil	Packed with good fats and antioxidants, also acts as an anti-inflammatory; toss all your noodle and rice dishes with a few tablespoons
dark chocolate	Rich in antioxidants; instant mood booster
cheese	Loaded with body-warming fat, some protein, and calcium

dehydrated lean ground beef	Satisfies carnivorous cravings with lean protein; mix with beans and rice for burritos or with instant mashed potatoes for a rib-sticking meal, or add to any noodle dish
whole grain pasta or brown rice	Great source of slow-burning complex carbs; the sky's the limit with recipe ideas
beans	Laden with low-fat protein and fiber
peanut butter	Jammed with protein and good fats
dried apricots	High in antioxidants, iron, potassium, and fiber; perfect for snacking or as an oatmeal topper

Chapter Six

Navigation

I firmly believe that some people are born with an innate sense of direction; others are hopelessly directionally challenged. But navigation is a critical skill that can be acquired. There's no excuse. If you're an outdoorsperson, you simply have to teach yourself the basics.

No matter what else you carry, a good topographical map is still your most essential navigational tool. *Fullerton Images*

THE GEAR

Unless you know how to use these items, there's simply no sense in carrying them. But once you do know how to use them, they're invaluable.

Maps. For anything other than a very straightforward hike on a well-marked, familiar trail, invest in a good map (stored in a plastic ziplock bag). A map

An array of navigational tools, clockwise from top left: topographical maps, Garmin GPSMap 62ST, Brunton O.S.S. 10B, iPhone. *Kristin Hostetter*

is, without a doubt, the most important navigational tool for hikers. There are plenty of excellent commercially available maps for popular locations (Trails Illustrated and other regional mapmakers), or you can order US Geological Survey (USGS) quads that cover anywhere in the United States. You want a map with contour lines, which give you a three-dimensional view of the surrounding terrain. Perhaps the best choice is to custom-design and print your own topo at a site like mytopo.com. You can center your map so that it incorporates your entire trip, choose the scale (see sidebar, page 56), choose certain finish options (like tear-resistant, waterproof paper), and have it shipped to your door in 24 hours.

Choosing Your Scale

Maps come in a variety of scales, and it's key to know what the scale represents so that you can choose the right one for you. In order to represent land features on a map, mapmakers must reduce them in size. The scale helps you understand how the ground distance relates to the detail you see on a map. Map scales are expressed through ratios, for example, 1:24K. The first number represents the unit of measurement on the map (often in inches or centimeters); the second number represents the same measurement on the ground. So every 1 inch on a 1:24K map equals 24,000 inches (2,000 feet, or 6.66 football fields) in the real world. The most detailed maps have lower numbers and are best for backcountry navigation because they give you more information on the terrain. For example, you can often see springs on 1:24K or better maps that would not be visible on 1:250K maps.

Liquid-filled compass. They come in all shapes and sizes, but they all do the same thing: point north to help get you oriented. They're inexpensive, foolproof, lightweight, and they never have dead batteries. Even if you rely on a global positioning system (GPS), it's always smart to pack a compass as a backup. The best hiker's models are the simplest. Look for a compass with a rotating bezel and a base plate with ruler markings. Unless you plan on getting into serious orienteering, you can skip the sighting mirrors and other fancy features. Recommended: Brunton O.S.S. 10B (bruntonoutdoor.com)

Digital compass. These are snazzy and easy to read, but because they require batteries and calibration, they're not as reliable as liquid-filled models. Plus, they're more expensive. I do not recommend digital compasses. There's a reason liquid-filled compasses have been around for so long. If it ain't broke, don't fix it.

GPS. GPS navigation is amazingly accurate because it uses satellite signals to triangulate your precise location. All GPS units allow you to collect a track, mark waypoints, navigate back to waypoints, and, if you've preloaded maps onto the device (see below), see your location within the terrain. But GPS devices are expensive, relatively heavy, and less effective in dense forest or deep canyons, and you're at the mercy of your batteries. Some GPS units come with such bells and whistles as built-in cameras or walkie-talkies, and you'll pay for these features in dollars and battery life. *Key:* Make sure your GPS is loaded with detailed maps. Some GPS units come preloaded (you'll pay more), but others require you to download them from the manufacturer's website (for a fee). It's worth it. The maps give you the context you need, allowing the GPS to focus on precision. Recommended: Garmin GPSMap 62ST (garmin.com)

Smartphone apps. Many phones can transform into fully featured GPS units with downloadable apps (for example, Backpacker GPS Trails or Backcountry Navigator). The biggest drawback to using your phone for navigation is that it sucks battery life, big time. That means you might not be able to make an emergency call when you really need to. ***Red flag:*** The market is completely saturated with apps, and a lot of them don't work when you leave town (and cell tower range) and head into the wilderness. For this reason, many of them (excluding the two listed above) are best for close-to-civilization day hikes.

Survival Smarts: Maintaining a Charge

When using your smartphone as a navigational tool, be careful to preserve battery life as much possible. Some tips:

1. Turn off the track log so the phone isn't constantly checking its GPS location.

2. Turn off the cellular and data signals so the phone isn't constantly searching for a cell or data signal.

3. Reduce screen size. You don't need to look at your screen every minute.

4. Pack a solar charger, many of which can eke juice from the sun even on overcast days. Recommended: Joos Orange (solarjoos.com)

Waterproofing a Map

Many commercial maps are printed on tear-proof, waterproof paper, which is a great feature. If yours is not, or if you printed it on regular computer paper, consider painting it (both sides) with a waterproofing agent, such as Aquaseal Map Seal. Always pack your map in a gallon-size ziplock bag as an extra precaution.

MAKING DO

What happens if your GPS batteries die, you lost your map, and/or you neglected to pack a compass? Keep your cool and use these skills, which you should practice every chance you get, whether you're driving in the car, walking the dog in the park, or on a hike.

Finding North

If you have a compass, it's easy. The arrow always finds north for you. But there are ways to find north even without a compass. Some are complicated, involving sticks in the sand and watch faces, math, and geometry. If you're just trying to get home, stick to the simple ways: watching the sun and stars.

Using the Sun

In the Northern Hemisphere, the sun rises in the east to southeast and sets in the west to southwest. (***Note:*** The exact direction of the rising and setting sun varies slightly during the course of the year as the sun takes a higher or lower path across the sky, depending on the season.) Use this information to orient your map, or at least maintain a consistent course as you navigate through the terrain. If you keep going straight, you will eventually hit a road. Remember this comforting thought: In the Lower 48, you are never more than 40 miles from a road; likely less than 10.

Using the Stars

You can get all fancy here if you happen to be an astronomy pro, or you can simply learn to locate the North Star. (Of course the weather doesn't always cooperate, but on clear nights, make use of the stars.) The Big Dipper is the most widely recognized constellation. Find it. Imagine a line connecting the two front stars that form the dipper, and follow that trajectory upwards. The first bright star you hit is the North Star. Mark that direction on the ground (with a stick or rock pile), and when the sun rises, use that information to verify north.

Everyone can spot the Big Dipper, right? This simplified image shows the approximate relationship of the North Star (the biggest, uppermost star here) to the Big Dipper. ©*Nicolas Raymond/licensed by Shutterstock.com*

Learn to Read Terrain and Orient It to Your Map

Topographical maps are gold mines of information. On practice hikes, look around you and constantly match what you see to the information on your map. Identify tall peaks, steep slopes (contour lines are close together), valleys and ravines (contour lines shaped like Vs), and flat areas (widely spaced contour lines). If you've lost your trail and are trying to find it or a road, think like an engineer, not a hiker: Roads aren't built over cliffs. Look for flat areas and wide riverbeds. As survival guru Cody Lundin says, rivers lead to people and cities.

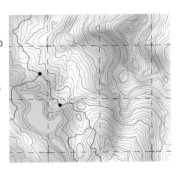

This image shows a gradual, then increasingly steep, climb up from the large lake on the left. Because the interval between each line represents a fixed change in elevation, when contour lines are close together, it indicates a steep slope. ©Kvadrat/licensed by Shutterstock.com

Use Darkness

When night starts to fall, make the decision to stay put, no matter what. Stumbling around in the darkness will get you nowhere and can lead to serious injury—the last thing you need. Find a good vantage point and scan the horizon. If you see any sign of light at all—like a vague pinkish glow in the sky that can signify a far-off town—mark the direction with a stick, a line of rocks, or an arrow drawn in the dirt. Then settle in for the night. When the sun rises, orient yourself, and head in that direction.

Survival Smarts: Keep Your Cool

In that moment when you realize you're lost, lots of things happen, and most of them aren't good. Your heart rate and respiration can spike; you quickly become confused, then panicky. The best thing you can do is pause for a moment, take some deep breaths, and try to chill out. People do stupid things when they panic. If you find yourself utterly, hopelessly lost, stay put. Find a spot that fulfills your shelter requirements, yet affords you some visibility that could lead to rescue, and settle in. Wandering cluelessly around in the wilds leads to exhaustion and just more confusion.

Survival Smarts: Communicate

I'm not a fan of leaving a note inside the windshield of my car, because I feel that's asking for a break-in. But hikers should always inform someone—a relative, friend, or ranger—before striking out into the bush. Tell people your plans and your intended route, and let them know when to expect you back so they can initiate a search if you don't return on time.

Chapter Seven

Knives

Hopefully you'll never have to use your knife for anything more dramatic than slicing salami, but if you ever get into trouble, it's arguably your very best resource. You'll use it for food prep, fire-making, shelter-making, gear repairs, first aid, and general MacGyvering. Every hiker knows: You just don't head off into the wilds without a knife.

A knife may be the single most useful tool a camper can carry. ©blueeyes/ licensed by Shutterstock.com

THE GEAR

Your choice of blades is very personal, based on how hard you'll use the knife, what sorts of tasks you anticipate, and your packing preferences. In all cases, look for a stainless steel blade that's at least 2.5 inches long and locks into place. The last thing you need out there is a severed finger.

Clockwise from top left: Blind Horse Maverick Scout (with leather sheath), Spyderco Manix2, Leatherman Juice S2. *Kristin Hostetter*

Multi-tool. There are a zillion to choose from in all weights and sizes and with different tool assortments. As a fix-it fanatic, I love a midsize multi-tool with scissors, small pliers, and a couple of screwdrivers. (Pliers are also very useful when you're cannibalizing unneeded things to create or improve useful ones.) But you often end up carrying tools you don't need. Look carefully at all the features and analyze their usefulness-to-weight ratio. Recommended: Leatherman Juice S2 (leatherman.com)

Fixed single blade. These Rambo-style knives are sturdy and burly and ideal for heavy woodcraft, such as processing wood for a fire. For true, hardworking survival situations, this is what you want. These knives require a protective sheath and take up more space than the other options. Recommended: Blind Horse Maverick Scout (blindhorseknives.com)

Folding single blade. Many hikers opt for this type of knife because it has few moving parts (and is therefore durable) and a large comfortable handle for rugged work, yet still folds up small for carrying. Recommended: Spyderco Manix 2 (spyderco.com)

KNIFE FEATURES

Knife lovers speak a unique language full of technical terms. Know these basic terms, and look for these features when shopping for a knife:

Tang. If you're shopping for a fixed-blade knife, look for one with a full tang. This means the metal extends from the blade all the way through the handle in one continuous piece. (The metal in the handle end is then sandwiched between the handle material.) A full-tang knife is far more robust than a partial-tang one. You can often (but not always) visually identify a full-tang knife because you will see the layer of metal throughout the length of the handle.

Blade shape. Blades come in many different shapes designed for different precise tasks. The most versatile and useful for hikers are drop-point and spear-point blades. Both these styles maintain a wide shape throughout the meat of the blade, with a quick taper at the end and a pointed tip. (A spear point has a symmetrical taper; a drop point is slightly asymmetrical.)

Single edge. For the most versatility, don't go for dagger-style knives. Opt for a blade with just one cutting edge, which will allow you to safely use the spine (see below) for batoning and fire-striking.

Flat spine. Look for a knife that has a solid, flat top edge (or spine) to it. Aside from the above-mentioned tasks, it also allows you to use the spine as a thumb rest (and for leverage) while cutting, carving, and processing tinder and kindling.

Serration. Serrated (or jagged edged) blades are good for sawing, cutting fibrous materials like rope or cardboard, or cutting flesh and bone. Many outdoor knives have a partially serrated blade, which is a smart alternative if you think you might find yourself in need of that type of cutting. But for general outdoor use, a straight blade is more versatile (and easier to sharpen).

THE SKILLS

Carving

Carving may seem like nothing more than a frivolous way to pass the time—until you realize you need more stakes for your tent. Practice good carving technique. Use your shoulder as well as your arm to power through cuts. Always cut away from your body, not toward it.

Snap Cutting

You may need to cut a small tree for a wading stick or to create a shelter. An ax is great, but when was the last time you packed one of those? A good knife

Snap cutting is an easy way to cut down smaller saplings. But only do this if you need to—if there's no deadfall around or you need a fresh, pliable stick rather than a more brittle dead one. Always pick a sapling that has several of the same species near it. *Joe Flowers*

will do the trick, as long as you know the proper technique. Bend the tree down, and start hard-carving at the top of the curve. Is the tree starting to splinter? Just keep cutting until you make it through the wood.

Scraping

While this technique tends to wear down your edge quickly, scraping dry woods at a 90-degree angle can yield super-fine dust and shavings that will readily take a spark.

Batoning

This technique is useful when trying to split wood for fire or shelter-making. Just set the knife's edge

Batoning is an effective way to split midsize logs, but beware. It will dull your blade, so be ready to get to work with a sharpener.
Joe Flowers

into the cross-section of the wood, then use a heavy object—like a rock or a small log—to gently hammer the spine of the knife through the wood lengthwise.

Ingenuity

Aside from the obvious cutting, you can do plenty of other things in the woods with a good knife:

- » Remove a splinter or cactus spine.
- » Hammer in a stake (using the handle).
- » Pry.
- » Make a spear for hunting.
- » Scrape rust off metal contact in an electrical device (like a light).
- » Open a can.
- » Dig.
- » Use as a screwdriver.
- » Drill a hole.
- » Use for notching.

Survival Smarts: Sharpening

A dull knife is almost as bad as no knife at all. Check the sharpness before each trip. (The blade should easily slide through a piece of paper.) If it doesn't, get to work with a whetstone. When you're in the field and using your knife hard, it can lose an edge quickly. But with a little practice, you can learn to field-sharpen your blade, even without a whetstone. Find a smooth, palm-size stone (river stones work well). Lubricate the stone with spit. Place your blade at about a 15-degree angle to the stone, and apply gentle pressure as you swipe the blade over the stone in a smooth, fluid, arc-like motion. Make about thirty passes, then flip the blade over and do the same on the other side.

Practice sharpening at home on your kitchen knives. ©*jps/ licensed by Shutterstock.com*

Chapter Eight

Illumination

Even if you're just headed out for a short afternoon hike, pack a light source. If you trip and snap your ankle, you'll have plenty of survival issues to deal with, and light shouldn't be one of them. Today's LED (light-emitting diodes) lights are so bright, so long-lasting, and so tiny, there's just no excuse for getting left in the dark.

LED headlamps are the most versatile lighting option for hikers and backpackers. *Fullerton Images*

THE GEAR

Types of Lights

Headlamps. Headlamps are the ideal survival lights because they allow you free use of your hands, and if

Clockwise from top: Fenix P2D, Black Diamond Orbit Lantern, Nite Ize BugLit, Petzl Tikka Plus 2, UCO Original Candle Lantern. *Kristin Hostetter*

you're in survival mode, you are most certainly multi-tasking. They're also compact and lightweight. Recommended: Petzl Tikka Plus 2 (petzl.com)

Flashlights. Available in so many shapes and sizes, flashlights are fine too. Good, tactical flashlights can be extremely bright and durable, and some are no bigger than a tube of Chapstick. Recommended: Fenix P2D (fenixlighting.com)

Mini auxiliary lights. Tiny keychain or squeeze lights are virtually weightless, so there's no reason not to always have one on you as a backup. Recommended: Nite Ize BugLit (niteize.com)

Lanterns. Think of these as luxury items. They're great around camp and in tents because they provide ambient light and often a nice, romantic glow. Example: Black Diamond Orbit Lantern (blackdiamond equipment.com)

Candles. If all else fails, a little candle is certainly better than nothing, and it can provide a surprising amount of heat if you're huddled under a reflective survival blanket.

Candle lanterns. Sometimes the occasion calls for flickering candlelight. These old-school candle lanterns are sturdy and fun. Of course they're also heavier and bulkier than electrical devices and don't throw off a whole ton of light. But they do set the mood. Recommended: UCO Original Candle Lantern (industrialrev.com)

Rechargeable Lights

Think about all the AA batteries you've burned through over the years. Probably enough to fill a 50-gallon drum. Rechargeable lights will not only save your conscience but will also save you some coin. However, lights still burn longer on disposable alkaline or lithium batteries, so rechargables are best for shorter trips. Your best bet might be lights that can run on either, like the Black Diamond ReVolt headlamp (blackdiamondequipment .com). That way you can go green for overnights or short, weekend trips and then pack extra disposables to use in case of emergency or for longer adventures.

Light Features

All lights are not created equal. Check this list of available features to decide which ones are right for you.

LED (light emitting diode) bulbs. There's a reason that virtually all lights available today are LEDs. They're more rugged and foolproof than other types of bulbs, and they last way longer. You may have some dinosaur incandescent flashlights lying around your house, which is fine, but don't bring them into the woods.

Brightness adjustment. Lights that allow you to set them on low will conserve power. Full-on search beam brightness isn't necessary for most camp tasks, so make sure to dim your light whenever you can.

Focusable/adjustable beam. The most versatile lights let you convert from a wide-angle beam, otherwise known as a proximity light, to a more focused spotlight. Proximity lights are ideal for around camp and in tents; spotlights are best for night hiking because of their extended reach and focused beam.

Regulated/nonregulated. Regulated lights are engineered to maintain a steady, consistent flow of light over a given time. Once that time is up, the light drops noticeably into "survival" mode. Nonregulated lights will steadily decrease in brightness over time.

Flasher mode. A blinking light is easy to spot from a great distance, and it's a well-known signal for help.

Waterproof housing. Look for gaskets around all the buttons and openings to keep water from trashing your light source.

Red or green mode. When you use a red or green light, your night vision isn't jeopardized once you turn the light off (or it runs out of juice). This isn't necessary, but it's a nice feature to have.

Lumens

Lumens measure light output, and all lights have lumen ratings so you can compare brightness. Ten lumens equal the light from one candle from 1 foot away. You'll find mini headlamps that start at 15 or so lumens and others that blast 150 lumens or more. For general camp/hiking use, somewhere around 70 lumens is ideal.

Batteries

When you're standing in front of the battery rack at the store, you'll see two main types of batteries: alkaline and lithium. Alkalines are cheaper at the register, but for serious outdoor use, lithium batteries are better. They last longer, perform better in colder temperatures, and are lighter (up to 30 percent) than alkalines.

Please dispose of your used batteries properly. Check with your town or city hall for local regulations. ©pryzmat/ licensed by Shutterstock.com

Skill: Signaling for Help

The universal SOS signal (which can be used with sound or light) is three short bursts (this means "S"), three longer bursts (about 2 seconds each) for the "O," followed by three more short bursts. Another good bet: Use the flasher mode found on most lights. A continuous, steady strobe is visible from great distances. To signal a plane or helicopter that you are OK, draw circles on the ground with your light.

Survival Smarts: Saving Battery Juice

Many flashlights and headlamps come with a lock feature that prevents accidental turn-ons inside a crammed pack. If yours doesn't, take precautionary steps to make sure your batteries aren't drained when you need them most. Whatever you do, don't reverse the orientation of the batteries inside the housing. This can result in a short circuit that will ruin your light. Instead, just remove the batteries and pack them separately, or place a piece of duct tape over the on/off switch to protect it from getting bumped inside your pack. When you're using your light, always go with the dimmest setting you can get away with. Lights that are on full blast burn through batteries substantially faster than those on a dimmer setting.

Chapter Nine

First Aid

On the majority of my wilderness trips, my first-aid kit sits at the bottom of my pack and never sees the light of day. And that's just the way I like it. But would I ever decide to jettison it to save a few pounds? No way. The reward is just not worth the risk. Bottom line: When you venture into the wilds, someone in your group—not everyone needs to carry one—should have a well-stocked first-aid kit.

You can improvise a splint using a foam sleeping pad and some tape. *Fullerton Images*

READY-MADE KITS

These come in a huge array of sizes, from palm-size ones that include little more than a few bandages to encyclopedia-size expedition kits that are loaded with supplies to handle everything short of open-heart surgery. Choose the right size kit for you based on the following criteria:

>> number of people in your group
>> remoteness of your trip
>> duration of your trip
>> types of activities

First-aid kits come in sturdy nylon zippered cases (some of them are waterproof), which is a nice way to stay organized. But if you have a well-stocked medicine cabinet at home and a freezer-weight zip-lock bag, you can build your own kit to save money and weight. Here are some key ingredients to pack. Amounts will vary depending on the above criteria.

>> adhesive bandages (variety of shapes and sizes)
>> sterile gauze pads
>> Steri-strips (for closing wounds)
>> ACE bandage (for sprains and compressing wounds)
>> medical or athletic tape
>> duct tape (store it wrapped around your trekking pole or water bottle)

- » blister treatment of your choice: moleskin, Second Skin (spenco.com), or Glacier Gel (adventuremedicalkits.com)
- » needle-nose syringe (for irrigating wounds)
- » povidone-iodine (antiseptic)
- » antibiotic ointment (like Neosporin or Bacitracin)
- » non-latex gloves
- » pain medication (acetaminophen, ibuprofen)
- » antihistamine (Benadryl)
- » diarrhea medication (Imodium)
- » antibiotics
- » tweezers (for removing ticks, splinters, and cactus spines)
- » water treatment tablets or drops like Potable Aqua (potableaqua.com), MSR Aquatabs (cascadedesigns.com), or Aquamira (aquamira.com)

Note: Be sure to replenish supplies directly after each trip. Don't wait till you're packing up for your next one in a hurry, because you'll forget which items you used the last time.

Kid Care

When traveling with your kids, it's always best just to assume someone will come down with something. Because if you don't pack kid-friendly meds, they surely will get sick. Bone up on their current dosages (based on weight), and stash a good supply of chewable ibuprofen and acetaminophen in your kit. Also a good bet: a soothing bug-bite balm, like AfterBite (tendercorp.com).

KNOW-HOW

If you spend a lot of time in the outdoors, and especially if you often travel with your family or lead groups of friends, do yourself and your loved ones a favor: Take a wilderness first-aid or, better yet, a wilderness first responder (WFR) course. A Google search will lead you to plenty of options all around the country. The Red Cross offers them, as do the National Outdoor Leadership School (NOLS), Wilderness Medical Associates, and many more. Make sure your CPR skills are up to date. And invest in a good first-aid manual so that you know the basics of patient assessment, wound management, fractures or breaks, shock treatment, etc.

At wilderness first-aid courses, you'll learn how to assess, treat, and evacuate victims safely.
©*Greg Epperson/licensed by Shutterstock.com*

IMPROVISING

Find yourself short on the proper materials? Check out these clever improvisations using common items in your pack:

Make a bandage. Cut thin strips off the hem of a cotton T-shirt; duct tape in place.

Disinfect a cut or burn. Smear honey over the wound and cover with gauze or cotton.

Clean a wound. Fill a ziplock bag with water, make a tiny hole in the corner, and squeeze water into the area to flush out dirt.

Ice an injury. Soak the area in cold creek water, or wrap it in a creek-soaked T-shirt.

Keep your hands clean. Improvise gloves by placing your hands in clean ziplock bags.

Calm your tummy. Mix two tablespoons of minty toothpaste with water, and drink.

Fashion a cervical collar for spine injuries. Roll a jacket into a tight tube and tie the arms around the neck.

Splint a broken bone. Wrap the area in a sleeping pad; secure with duct tape.

Chapter Ten

Sun Protection

Years ago I flew out to Colorado in July to hike a 50-mile section of the Continental Divide Trail. When I landed in sunny Colorado, I realized I had forgotten my sunglasses, so I stopped at a gas station and bought a cheapo pair for around 10 bucks. Bad idea. They looked legit, but when I came out of the mountains six days later, my eyes were so fried, red, and sore that they remained swollen and irritated for a week.

The sun can be mean, especially at higher elevations. While it's always nice to come out of the woods with a golden tan, you can do some serious damage to your skin and eyes if you don't pack the right gear.

Shades, a brimmed hat, and plenty of sunscreen are essentials, especially in alpine conditions. *Kristin Hostetter*

Clockwise from top left: Outdoor Research Helios Hat, Elemental Herbs sunscreen, UV Buff, Ex Officio Dryflylite long-sleeve shirt, Costa Del Mar Cat Cay sunglasses. *Kristin Hostetter*

SUN GEAR

Always pack the following items, whether you're headed out for a day or a week.

Sunglasses. Make sure they block 95 percent of UVA light and 99 percent of UBV radiation. Darkness—or visible light transmission—has nothing to do with protection. In fact, cheap, dark lenses can do more harm than good. (That was likely the cause of my issues in the Rockies.) That's because darker lenses allow you to relax your eyes; your pupils dilate and admit more radiation. You're better off squinting. Recommended: Julbo (julbousa.com), Revo

(revo.com), Smith (smithoptics.com), Costa del Mar (costadelmar.com)

Sunscreen. They are not all created equal. Ignore enticing terms like "all-day protection," "broad spectrum protection," or "PABA-free" (virtually all sunscreens avoid PABA because it irritates the skin). Read the active ingredients, and look for one or more of the following: titanium dioxide, zinc oxide, photo-stabilized avobenzone, or Mexoryl, all of which shield against UVA and UVB rays. Get a sunscreen with an SPF (sun protection factor) of 30, and reapply every 2 hours (more if you're swimming or sweating hard). The white, pasty look may not look so hot in photos, but that white sheen—from zinc oxide—is a very effective physical barrier to the sun. Avoid chemical spray-ons. They don't work as well and wear off quicker. Recommended: Elemental Herbs (elemental herbs.com)

Learn to love the pasty look. It comes from zinc oxide and means you're protected from the sun's harsh rays.
Kristin Hostetter

Clothing. Look for long-sleeved shirts and long pants made of thin, densely woven materials. Many companies now offer an SPF rating with their garments, which let you cross-compare the effectiveness of the protection. Light colors will keep you cooler; darker colors will absorb the sun and warm you up. Recommended: ExOfficio (exofficio.com)

Hat. Any brimmed hat will do, including your lucky baseball cap, but for the best protection, look for a wide-brimmed hat that will shield your ears and neck as well. Recommended: Outdoor Research Helios Hat (outdoorresearch.com)

A Buff (buffusa.com), a long tube of wicking material (comes in wool and several polyester versions), is a versatile way to protect your head from sun and cold. *Kristin Hostetter*

Bandanna. Place a cotton bandana under your ball cap for added neck protection, or invest in an extra-long neck gaiter made of sun-blocking material designed to wrap your head in countless ways. Recommended: UV Buff (buffusa.com)

MAKING DO

If you're caught without protection, here are a few tips for getting home without getting baked.

Make Duct Tape Glasses

Go without shades for a day on the snow, and you could find yourself with snow blindness, which is no fun. Essentially it's when your cornea gets a sunburn,

These may look bizarre, but they could save your eyes from serious strain or snow blindness. *Kristin Hostetter*

and it can result in intense pain, swelling, and tearing. If you lose your sunglasses, improvise with duct tape: Take an 18-inch strip of duct tape and fold it back over itself to form a 9-inch-long strip. Next, using the tip of a very sharp knife, cut a 4-inch horizontal slit in the center of the tape. Make another pass with the knife to remove a sliver of tape and make the slit slightly wider. (The slit should only be about the width of a tortilla chip.) Rig a headstrap using cordage or another length of rolled duct tape. You will look like a total dork, but you'll save your eyes a world of pain.

If you wear prescription eyeglasses, you can also turn them into emergency sunglasses. Just cut a slit into the tape, and place a piece directly over each lens.

How to Make a Shemagh from a Long-Sleeve Shirt

It's no surprise that people who live in desert regions have been using these headwraps since the beginning of time. They provide almost complete head and neck protection from the sun, and you can jury-rig one from any long-sleeve shirt. Just pull the shirt over your head and position the neck opening over your face. Leave the back of the shirt positioned over the top of your head. Take the sleeves and cross them over your mouth, tying them together behind your head. You can now adjust the size of the opening to cover everything but your eyes. Tuck the ends of the sleeves into the back of your shirt. **Tip:** In extreme heat, wet the material before making the shemagh. It will feel lovely and keep your body temperature low so that you avoid heat stroke.

Make a Mud Mask

If your sunscreen runs out or goes missing, go tribal. Find a mud puddle and smear any exposed skin. Mud acts as a physical barrier to the sun and will prevent you from getting burned. It will eventually dry and crack and should be frequently reapplied, but even the dirty residue it leaves behind will help protect you. You'll look like a Charlie Brown's buddy Pigpen, but at least you won't get fried.

Appendix: Resources

The best way to learn any outdoor survival skills is to enroll in a course and get your hands dirty. You'll learn how to build shelters, start fires, and turn found objects and garbage into useful tools. Most important, you'll build the skills and confidence that will help you keep a cool head if you ever find yourselves in dire straits.

Aboriginal Living Skills School. Led by barefooted survival celebrity Cody Lundin, ALSS specializes in teaching primitive outdoor survival skills in the wilderness of Arizona. Learn more at codylundin.com.

Willow Haven Outdoor School. This 21-acre survival training camp is located in Indiana. WHO offers survival and primitive skills courses ranging from one to three days, as well as online training courses. For more info contact willowhavenoutdoor.com.

Wilderness Medical Associates. WMA teaches comprehensive two-day wilderness medical courses around the country. Go to wildmed.com for course schedule.

NOLS. NOLS offers two-day wilderness medicine courses, as well as many other outdoor skills-based courses of varying lengths. Topics cover backpacking, climbing, mountaineering, and horsepacking. Learn more at nols.edu.

Red Cross. The Red Cross offers Wilderness and Remote First Aid Courses aimed at Scouts and Scout leaders. Go to redcross.org for more information.

REI. REI's Outdoor School features a wide range of one-day, affordable classes around the country on topics ranging from first aid to navigation and more. Check out rei.com for more details.

Bushcraft NorthWest. Located in southern Washington, Bushcraft offers small-size (eight people) classes focusing on shelter- and fire-building, knife skills, navigation, edible plants, and more. Go to bushcraftnorthwest.com to learn more.

Ozark Mountain Preparedness. This Arkansas-based wilderness skills school teaches both day and multiday courses on everything from cooking to fishing to shelter-building and trapping. Go to ozarkmountainpreparedness.com for more details.

Backtracks Primitive Skills Gatherings. These annual events take place in Idaho and Arizona and feature instruction, camaraderie, and evening campfire programs. Learn more at backtracks.net.

INDEX

ABOUT THE AUTHOR

Kristin Hostetter has been *Backpacker* magazine's gear editor since 1994. She has put thousands of camping and hiking products through *Backpacker*'s rigorous gear-testing program. Her travels have taken her all over the world—from Alaska to Iceland, from Wales to Wyoming, from Tasmania to

Fullerton Images

Tuckerman's Ravine—in search of the best testing conditions, which often means the worst weather! She has appeared as a gear expert on NBC's *Today,* CBS's *The Early Show,* and *The Martha Stewart Show,* among others. Kristin is the author of four other books: the National Outdoor Book award–winning *Complete Guide to Outdoor Gear Maintenance and Repair* (FalconGuides), *Don't Forget the Duct Tape, Adventure Journal,* and *Tent and Car Camper's Handbook.* Kristin is also known as the "Gear Pro" on backpacker.com, where she answers questions from readers about all sorts of outdoor skills and gear. She lives in Massachusetts with her husband and two sons, all of whom love to join Kristin on her adventures whenever possible.